This book belongs to:

Without your voice we don't exist.
Please, support us and leave a review

Thank you!

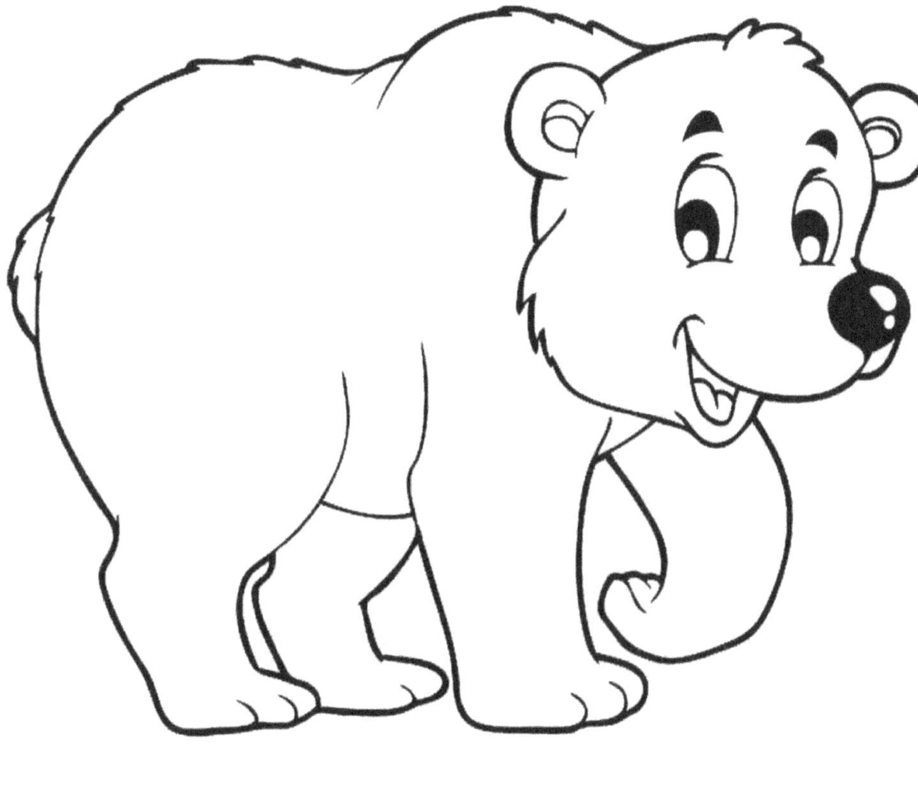

Bear

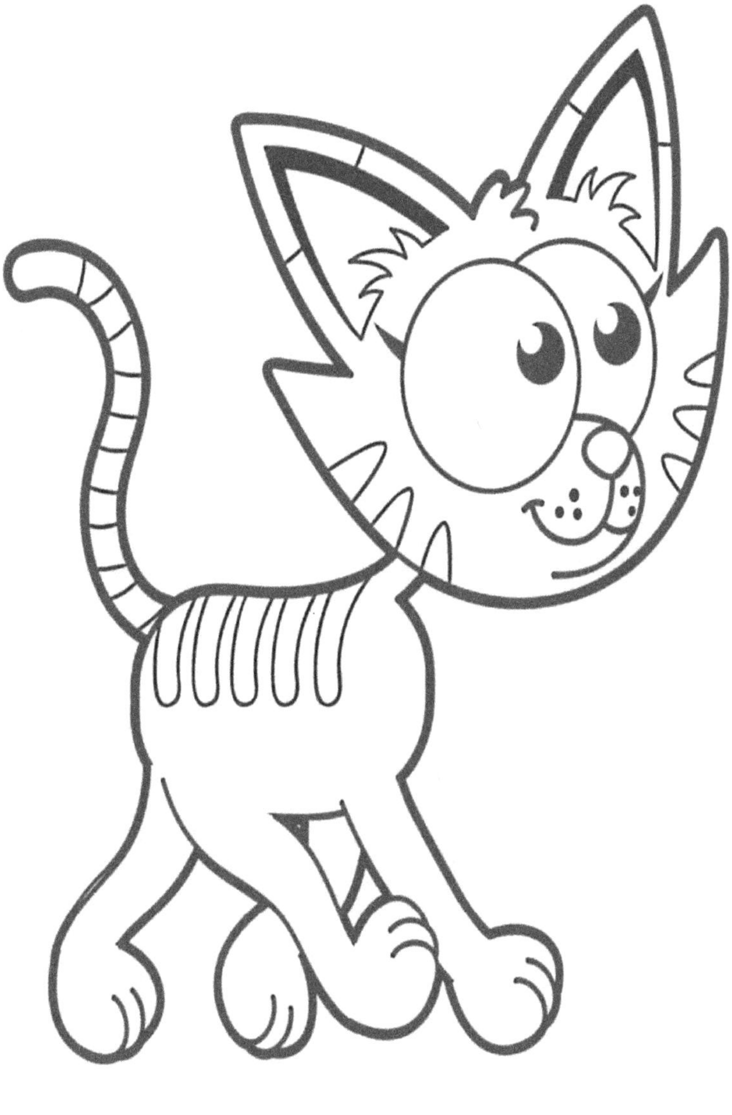

Cat

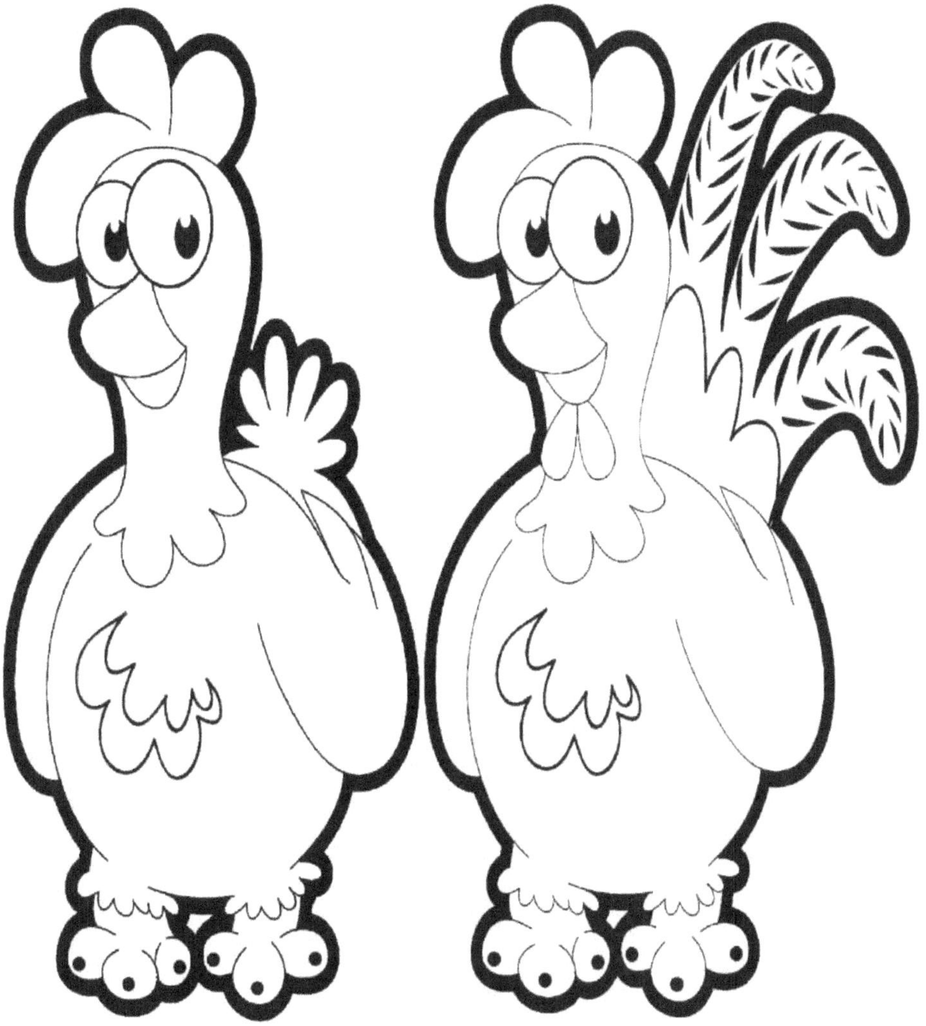

Chickens

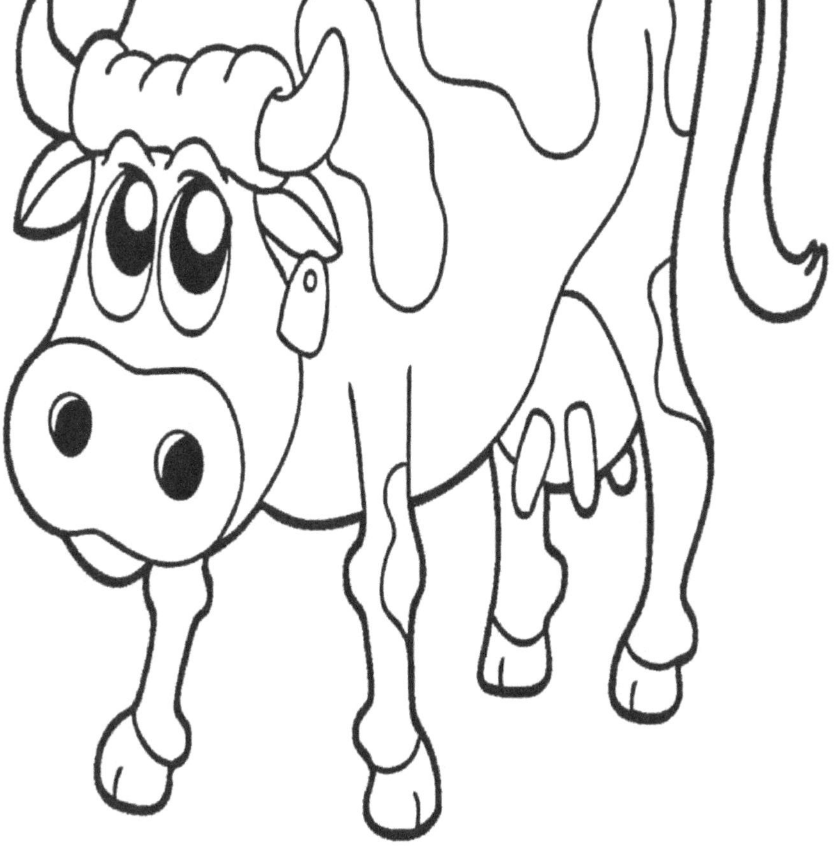

Cow

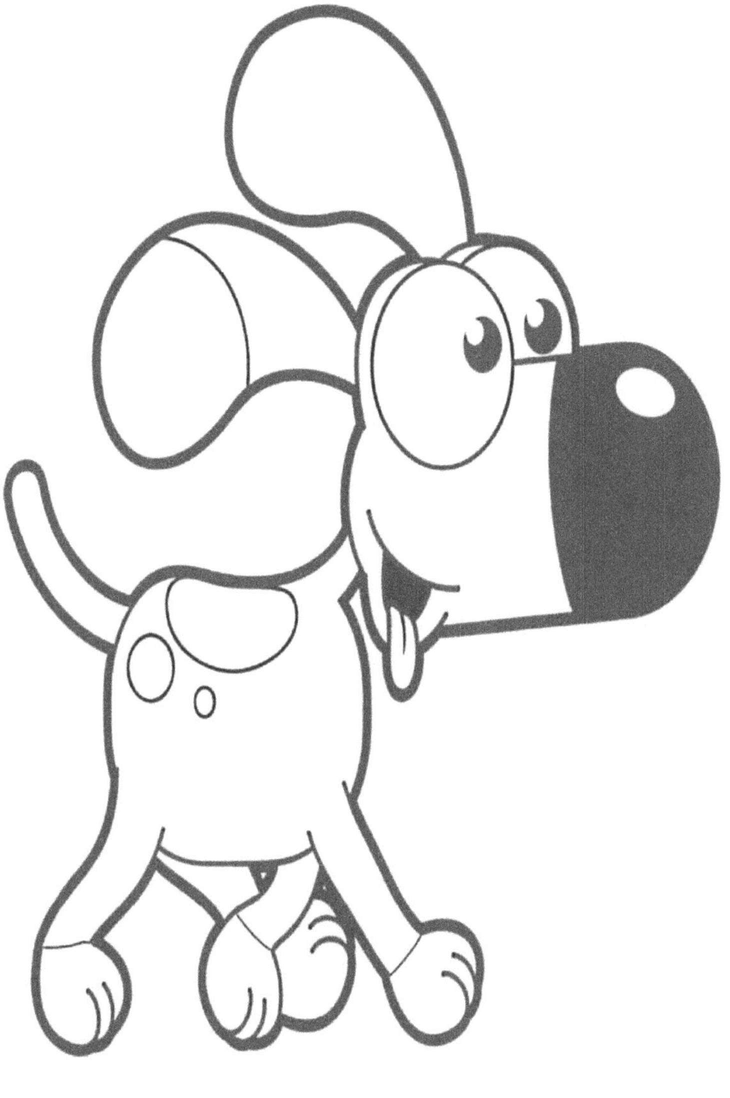

Dog

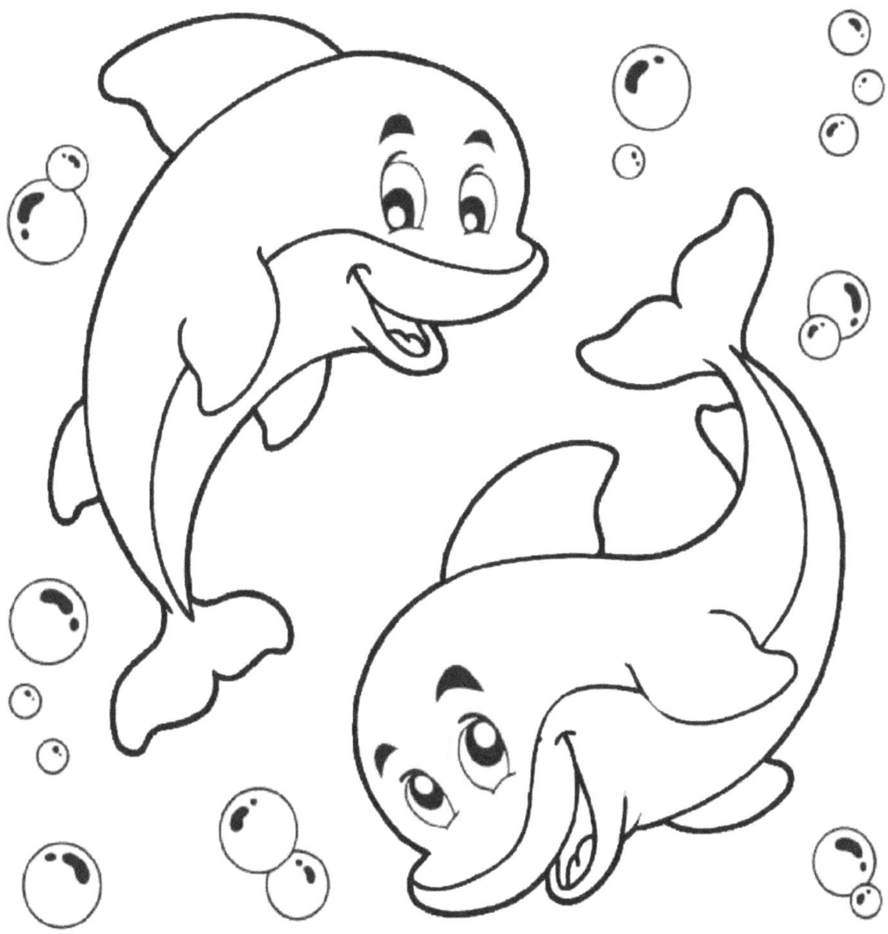

Dolphins

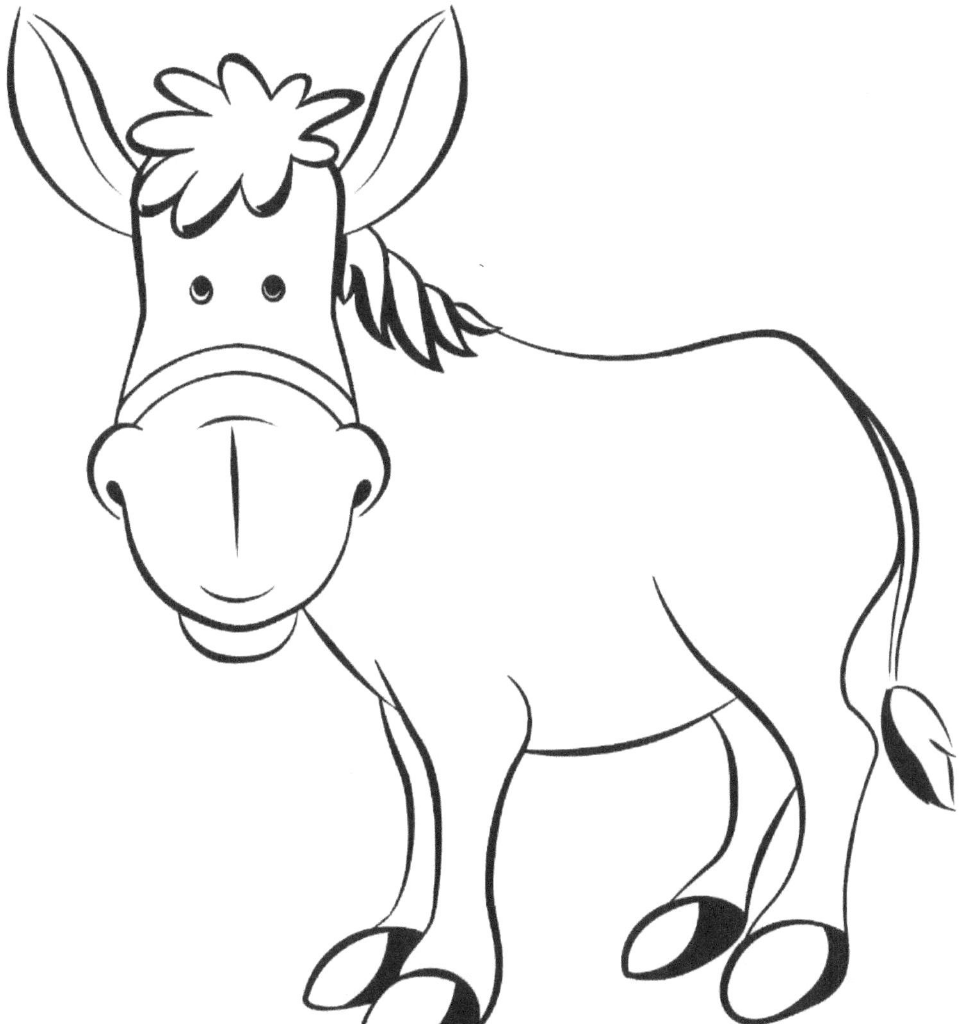

Donkey

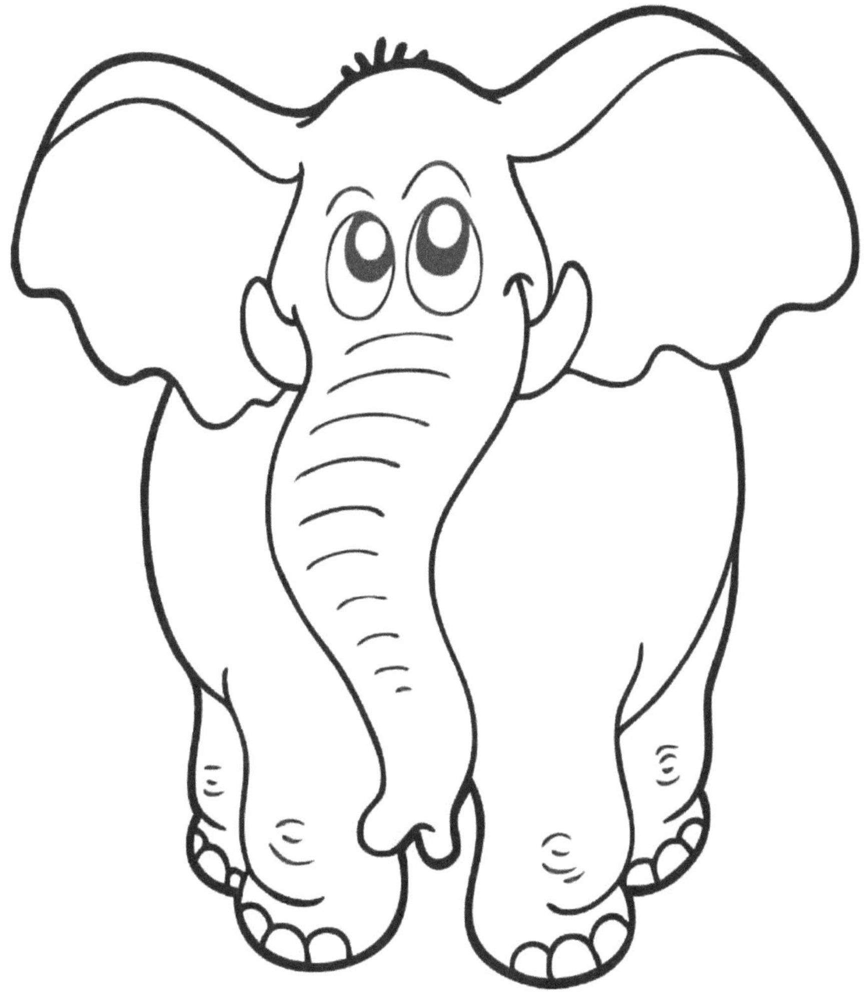

Elephant

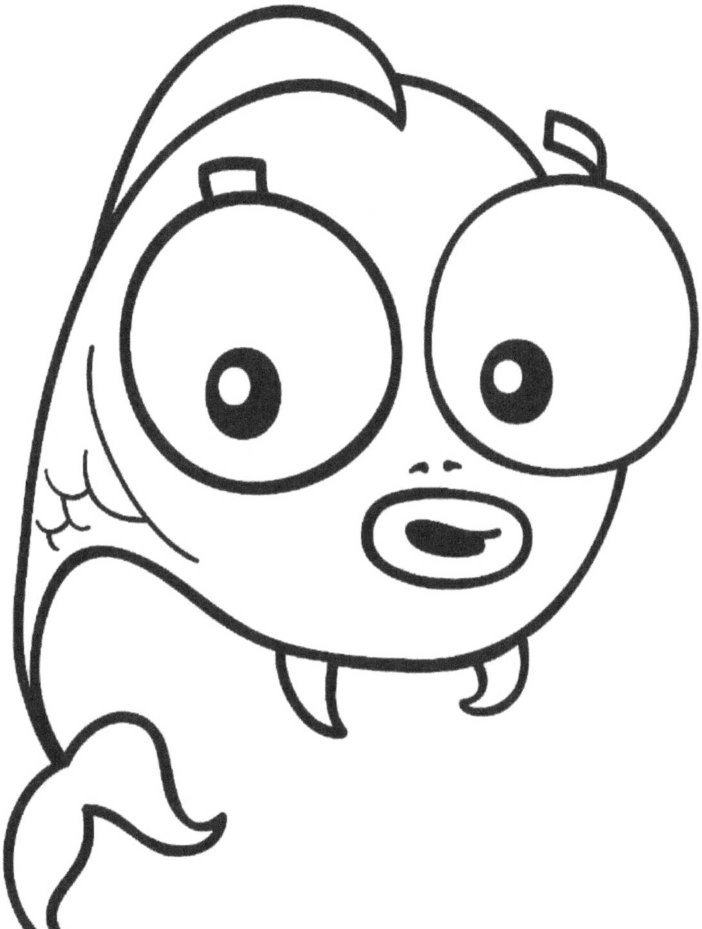

Fish

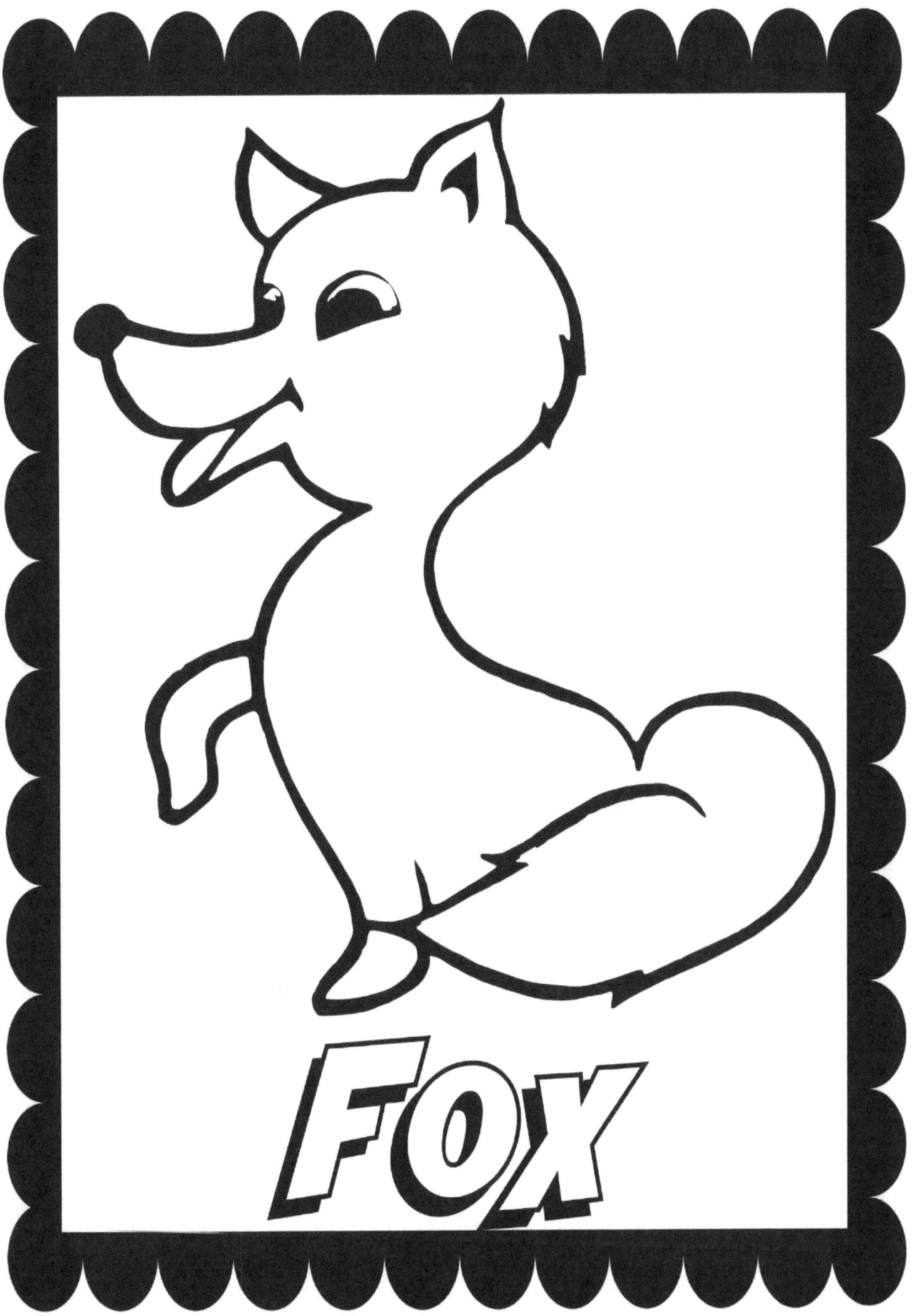
FOX

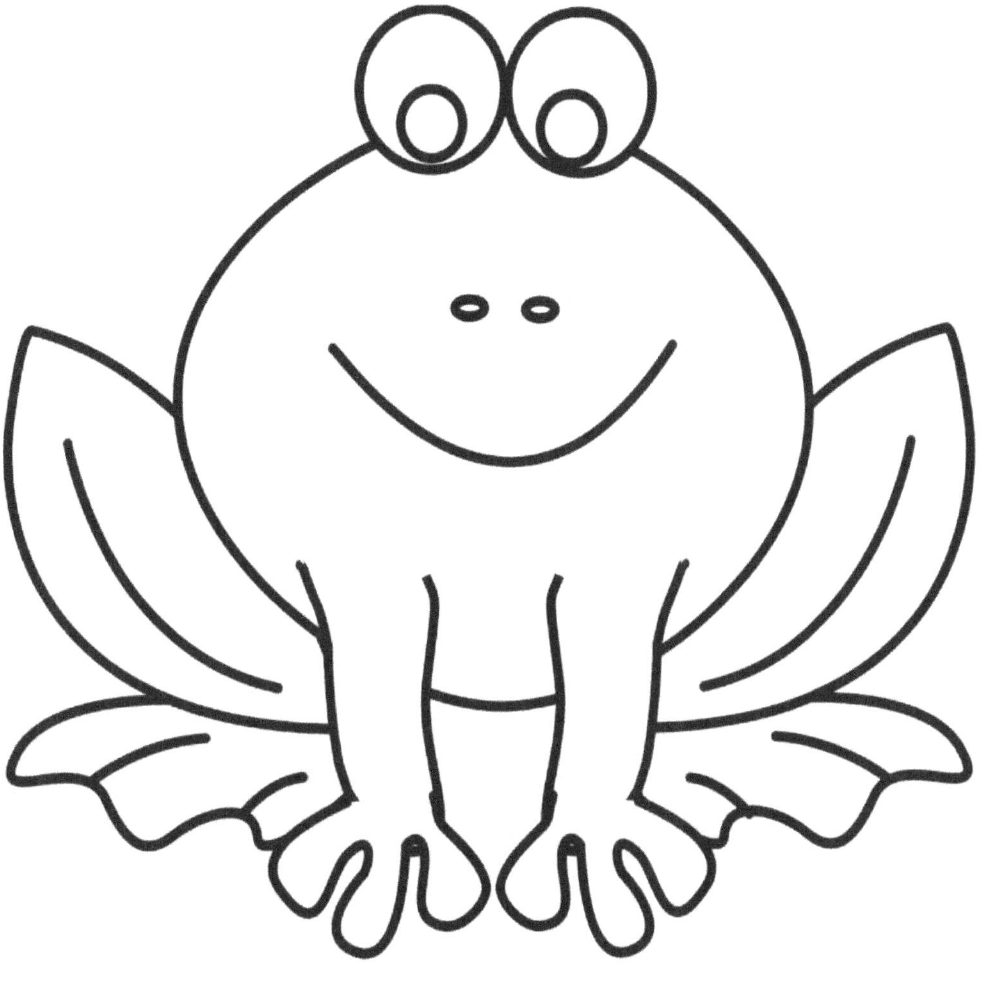

Frog

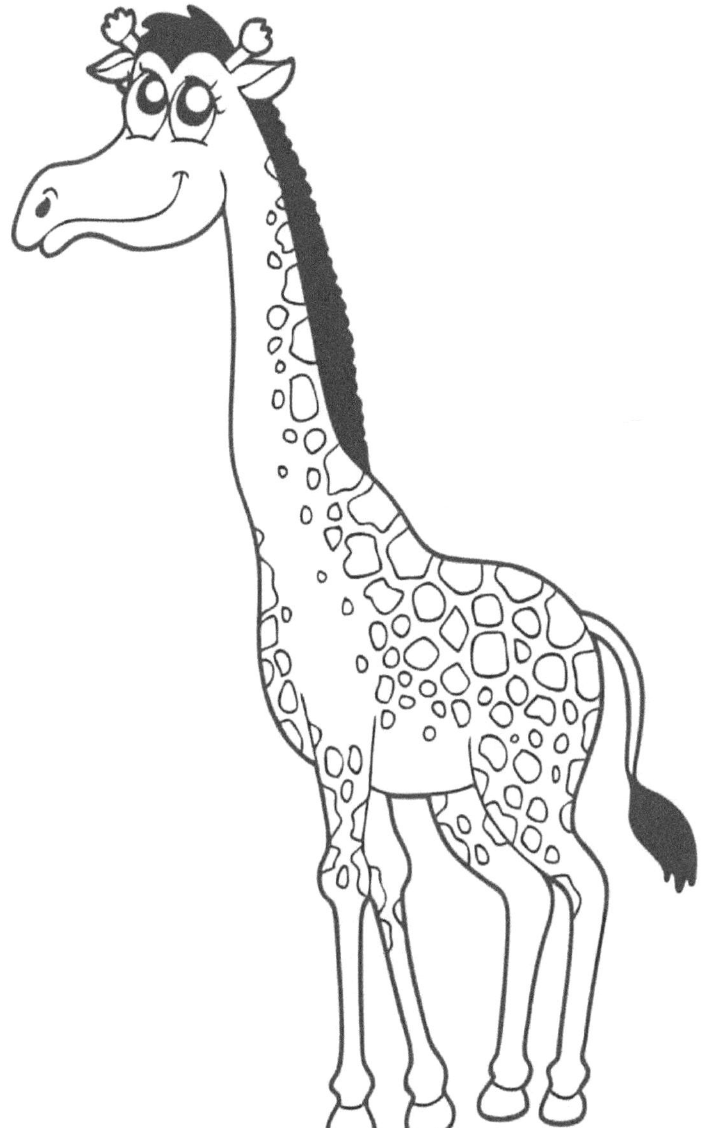

Giraffe

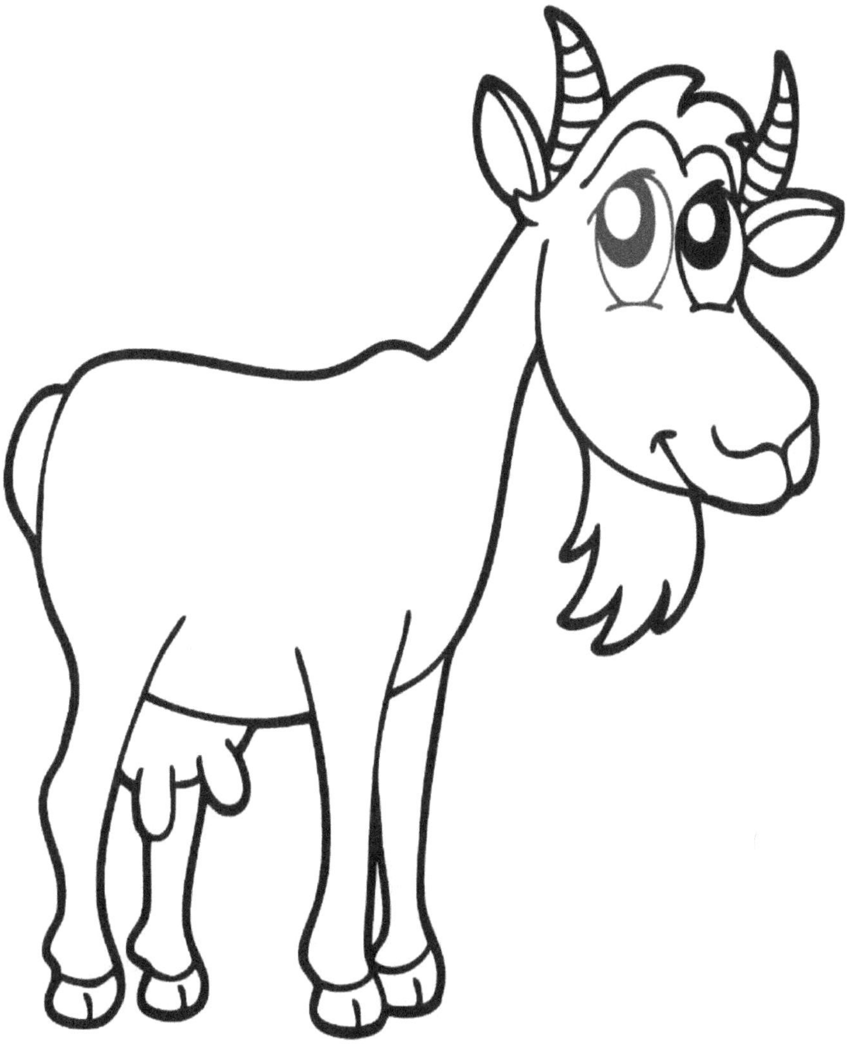

Goat

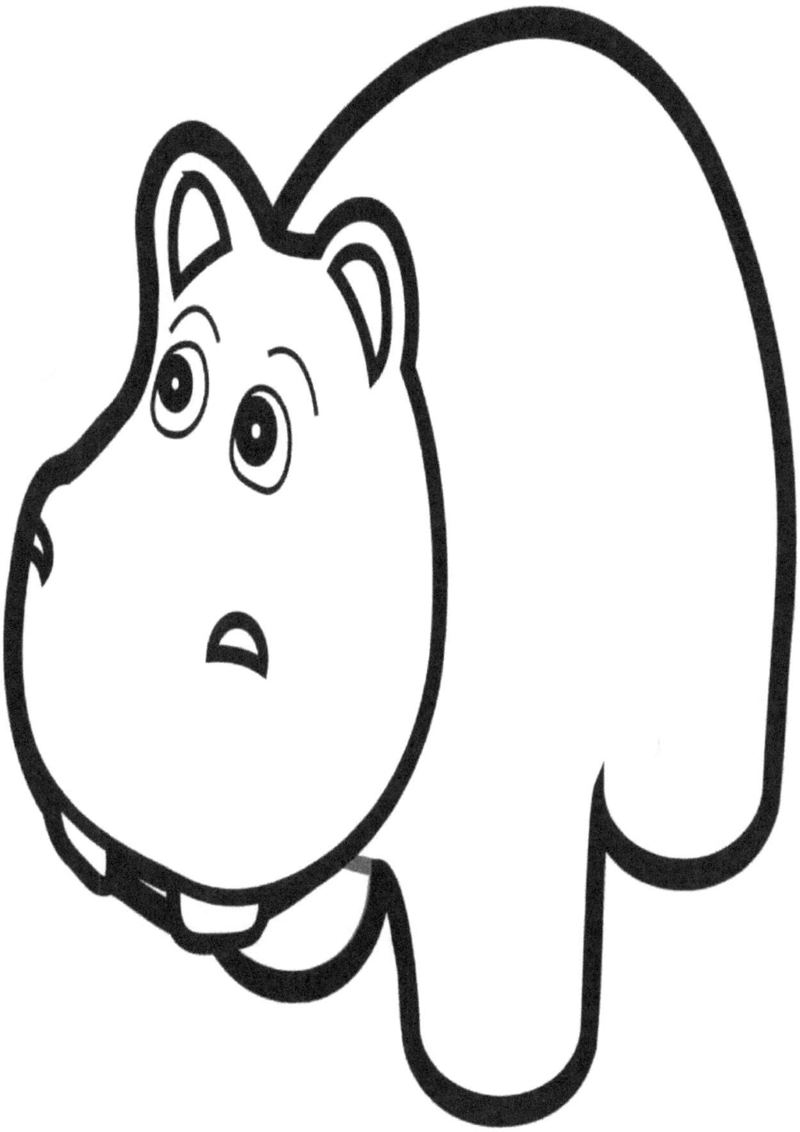

HiPPO

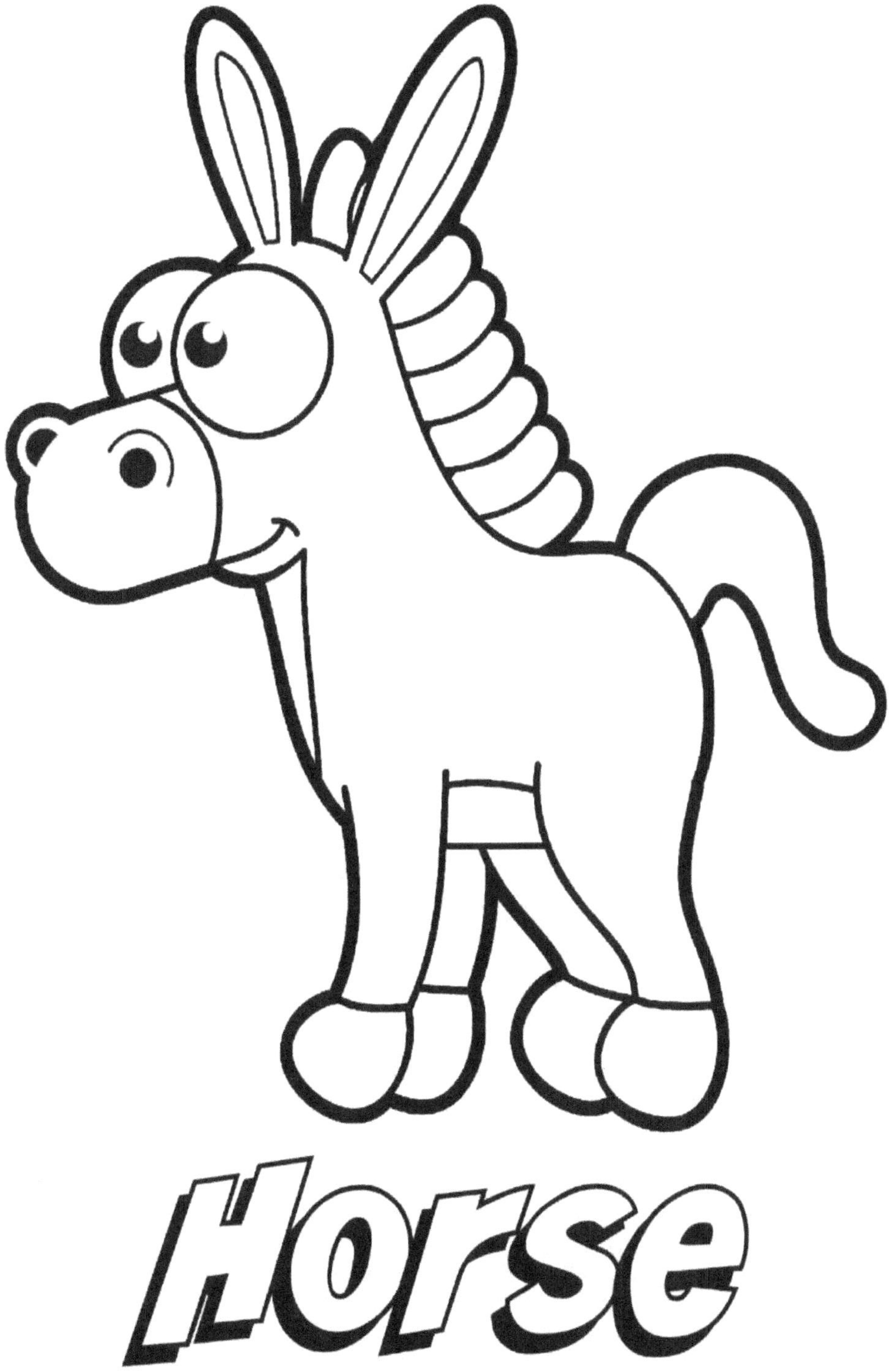

Horse

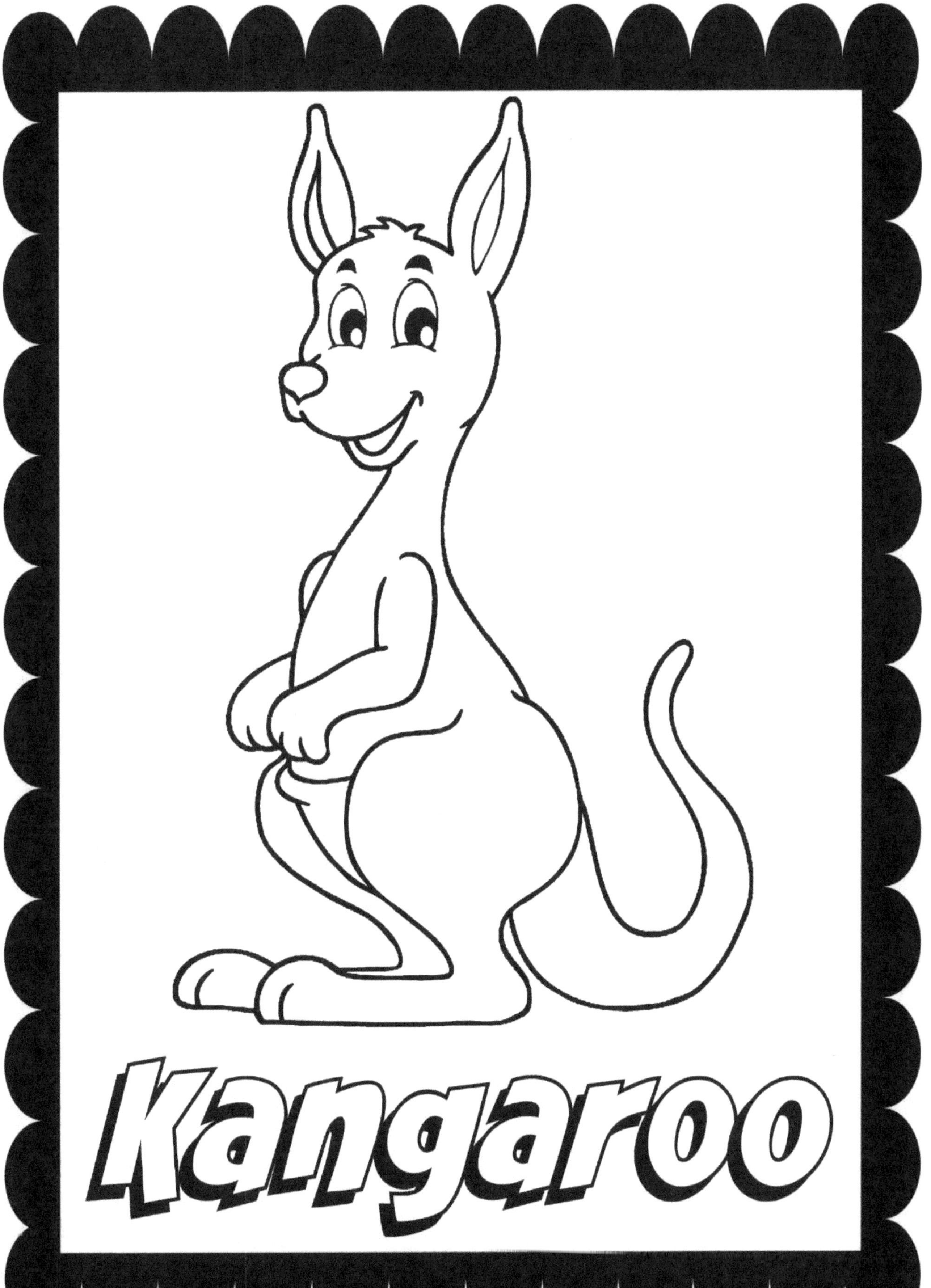
Kangaroo

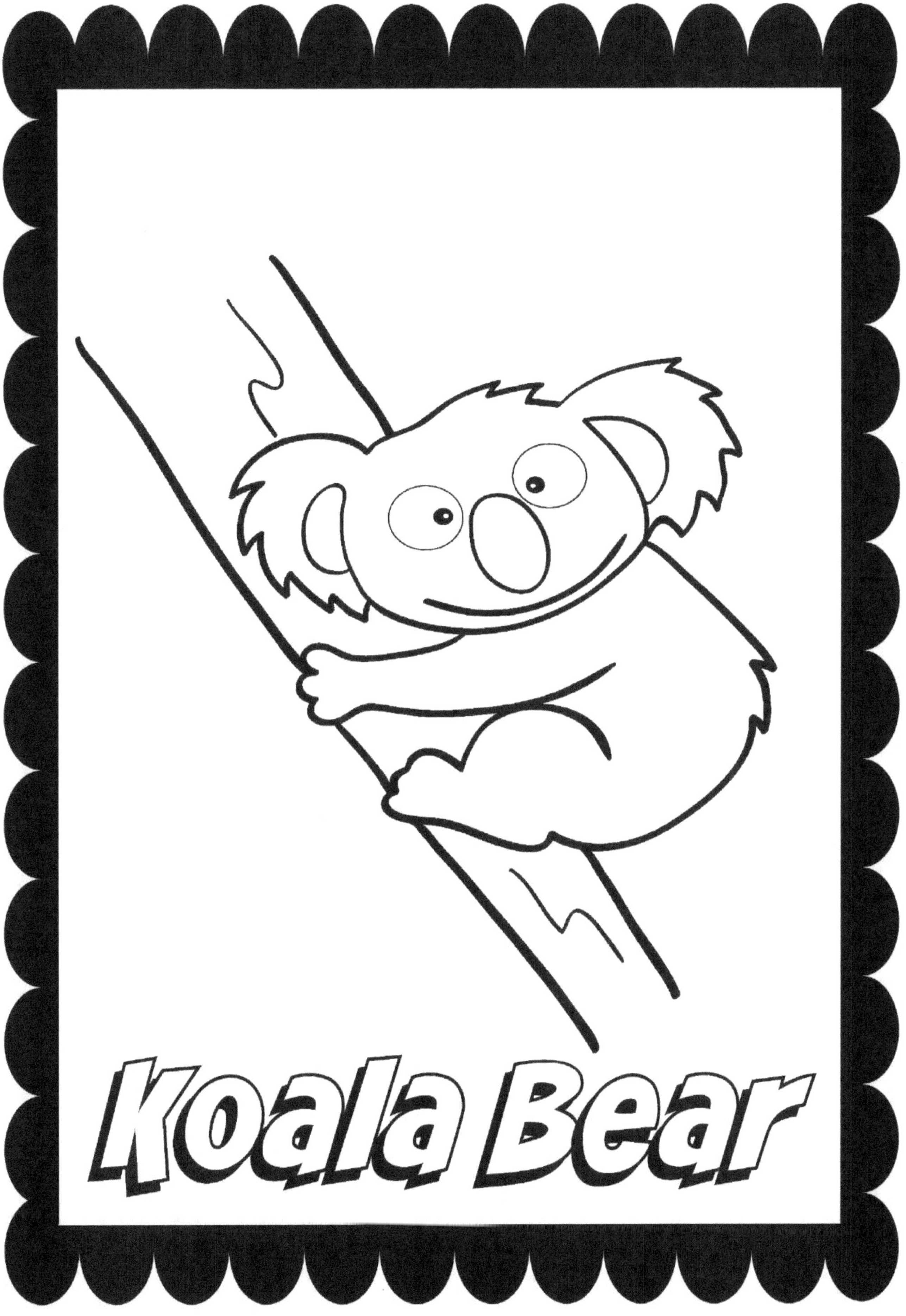
Koala Bear

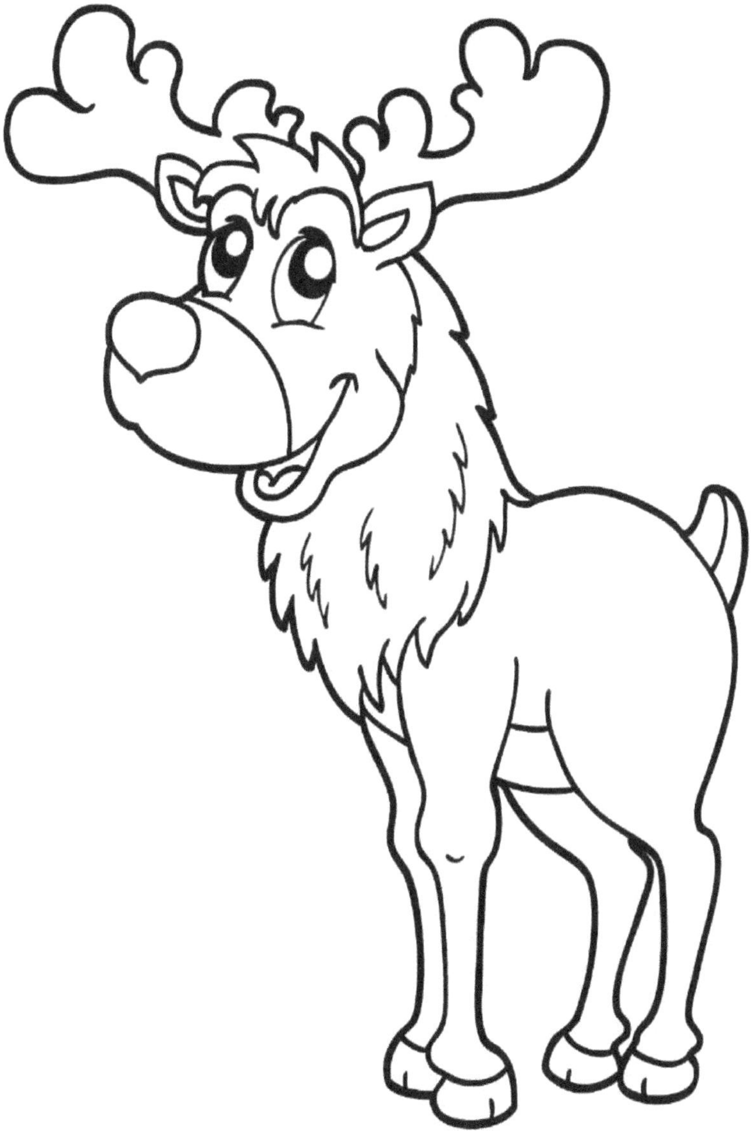

Moose

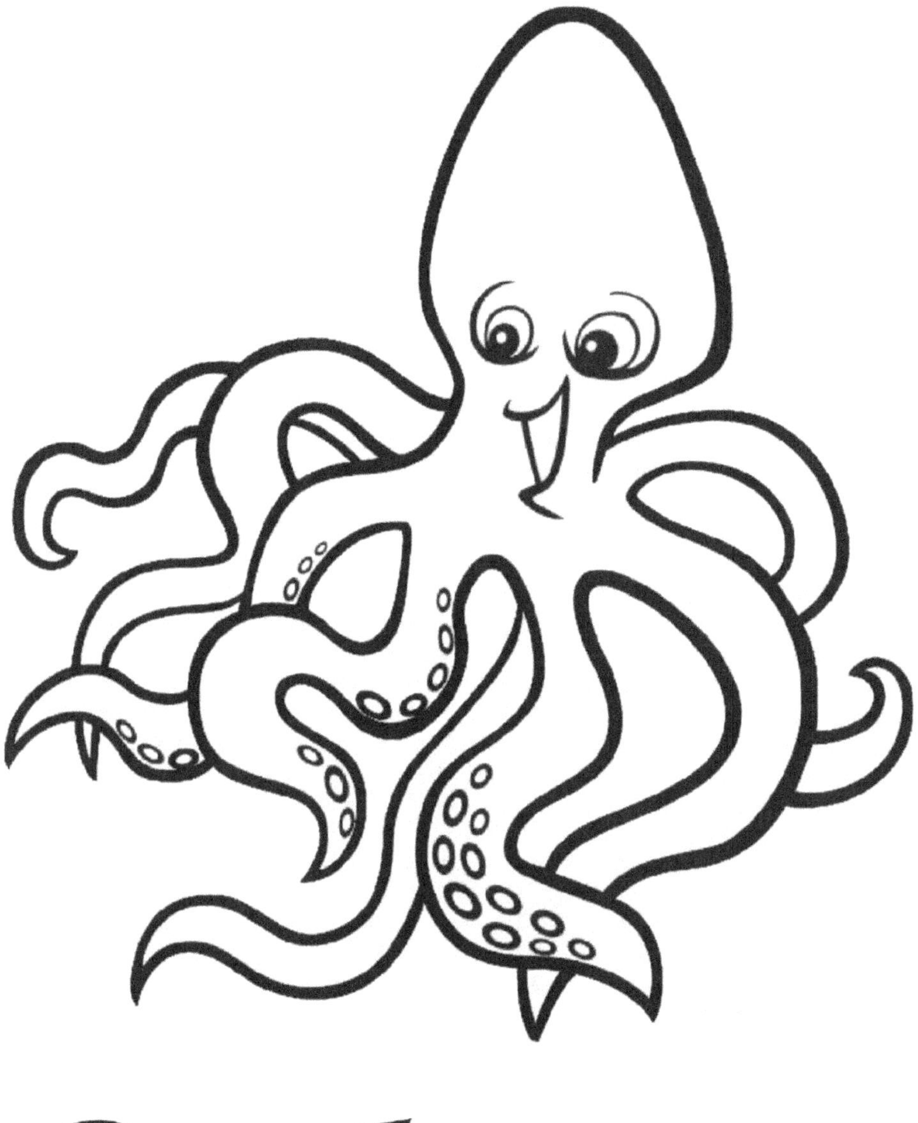

Octopus

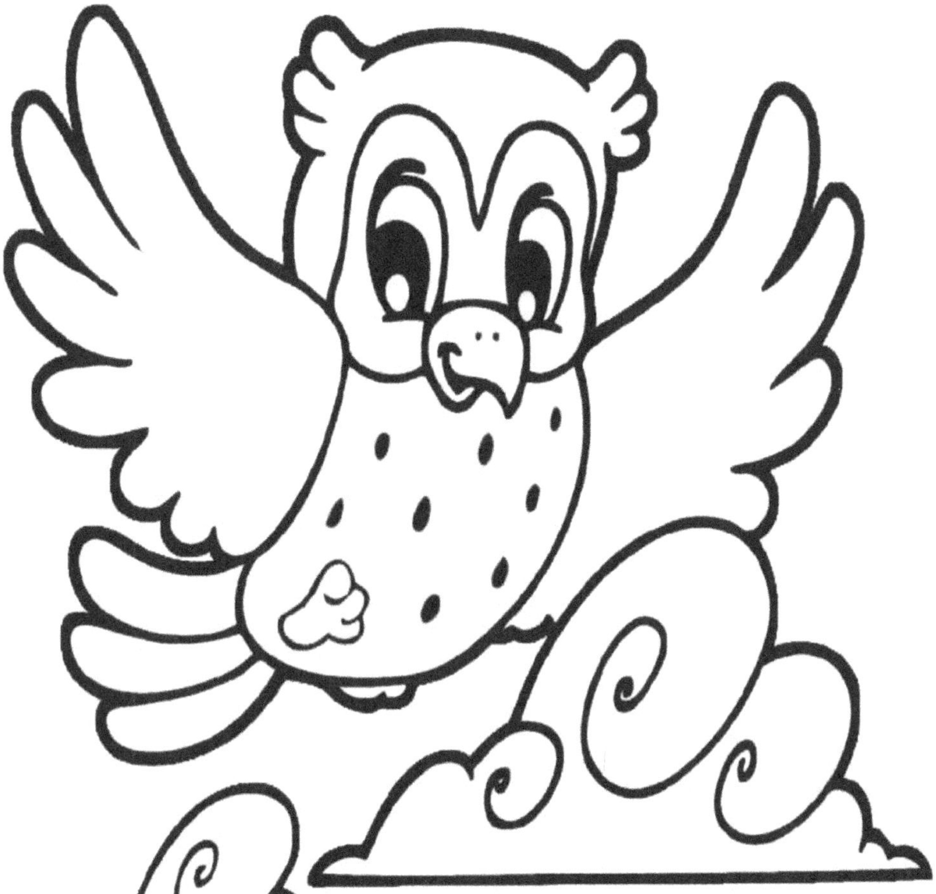

Owl

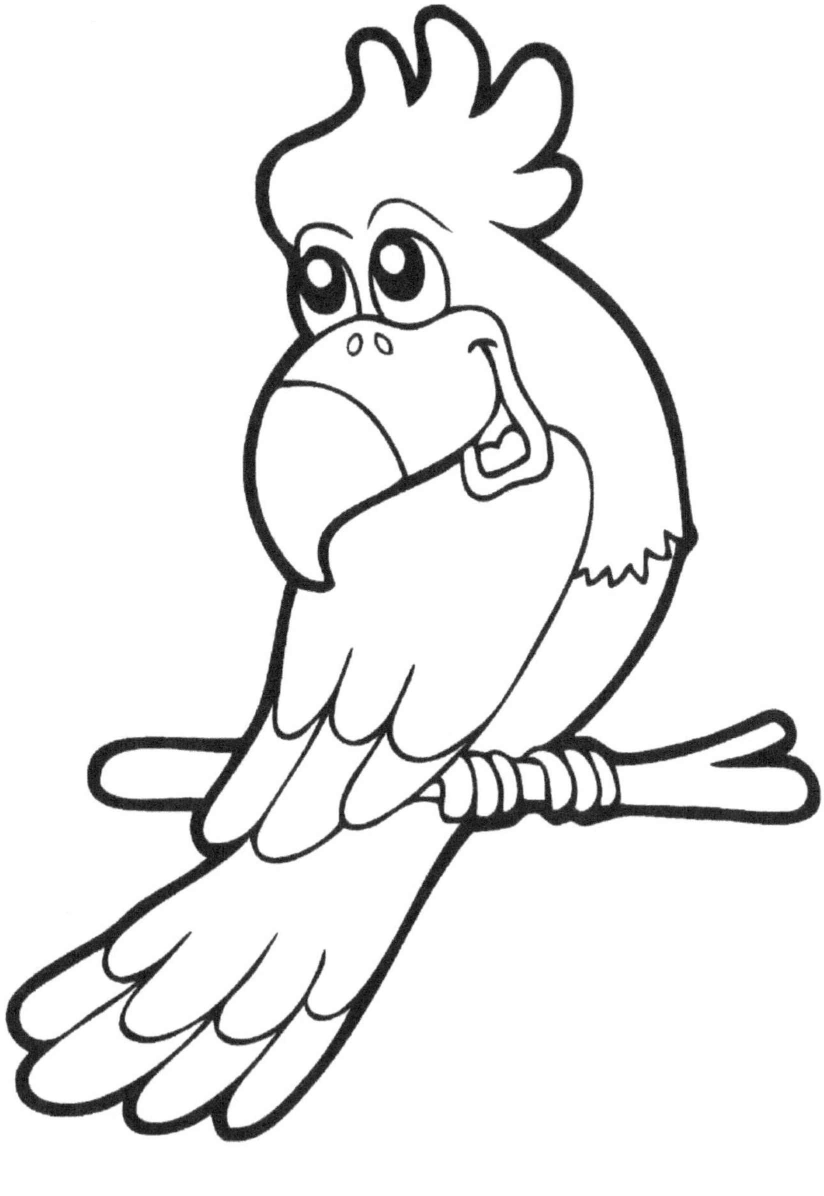

Parrot

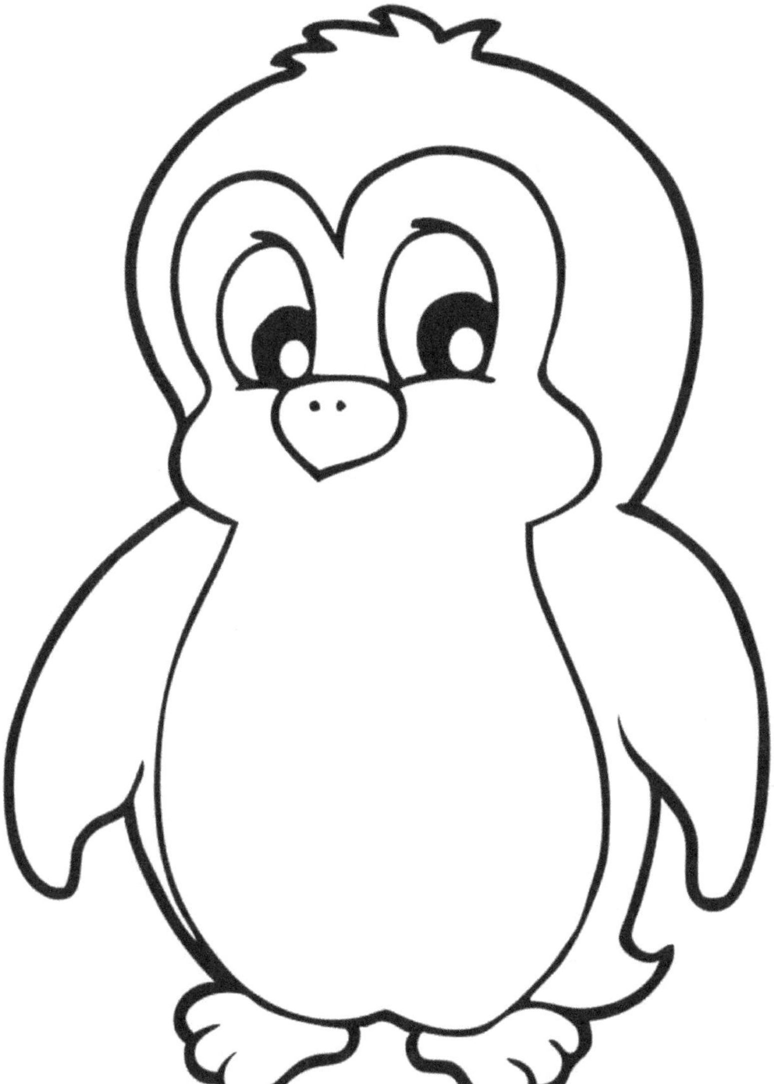

Penguin

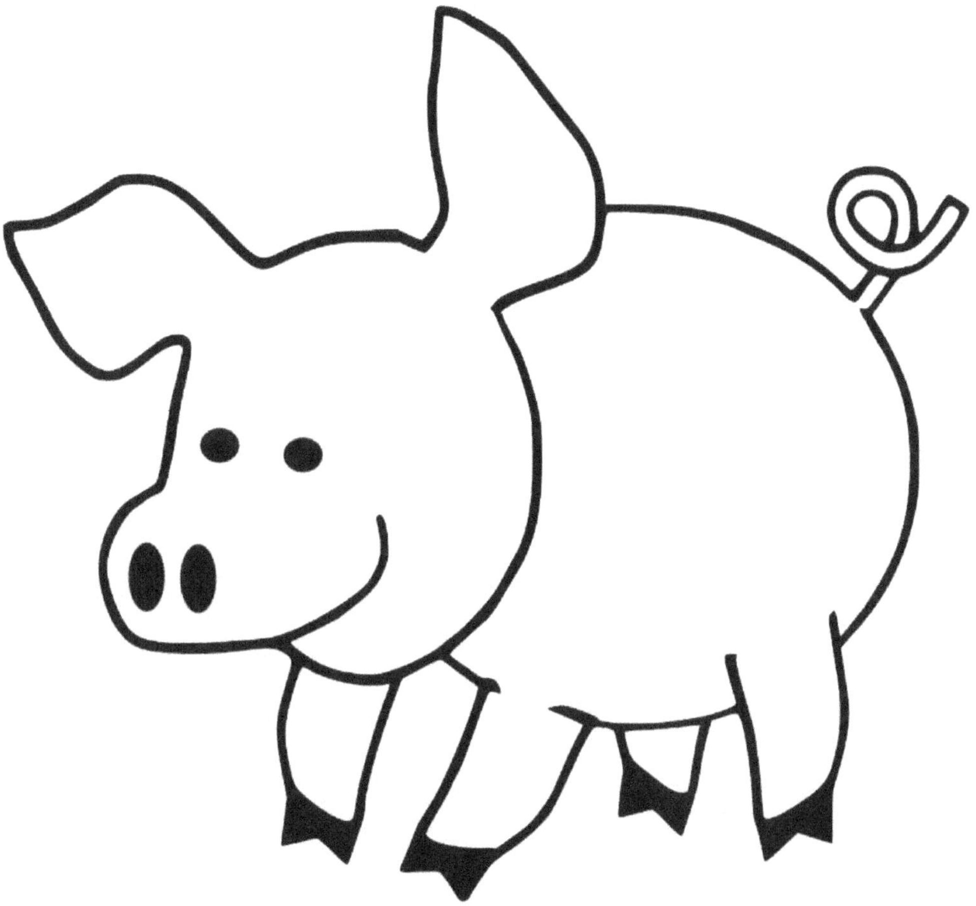

Pig

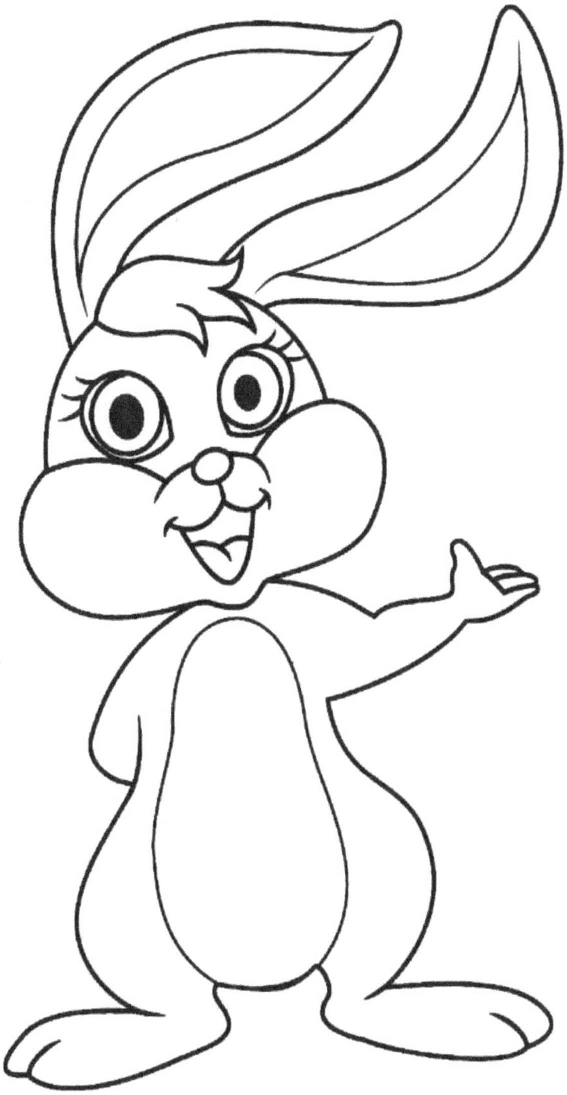

Rabbit

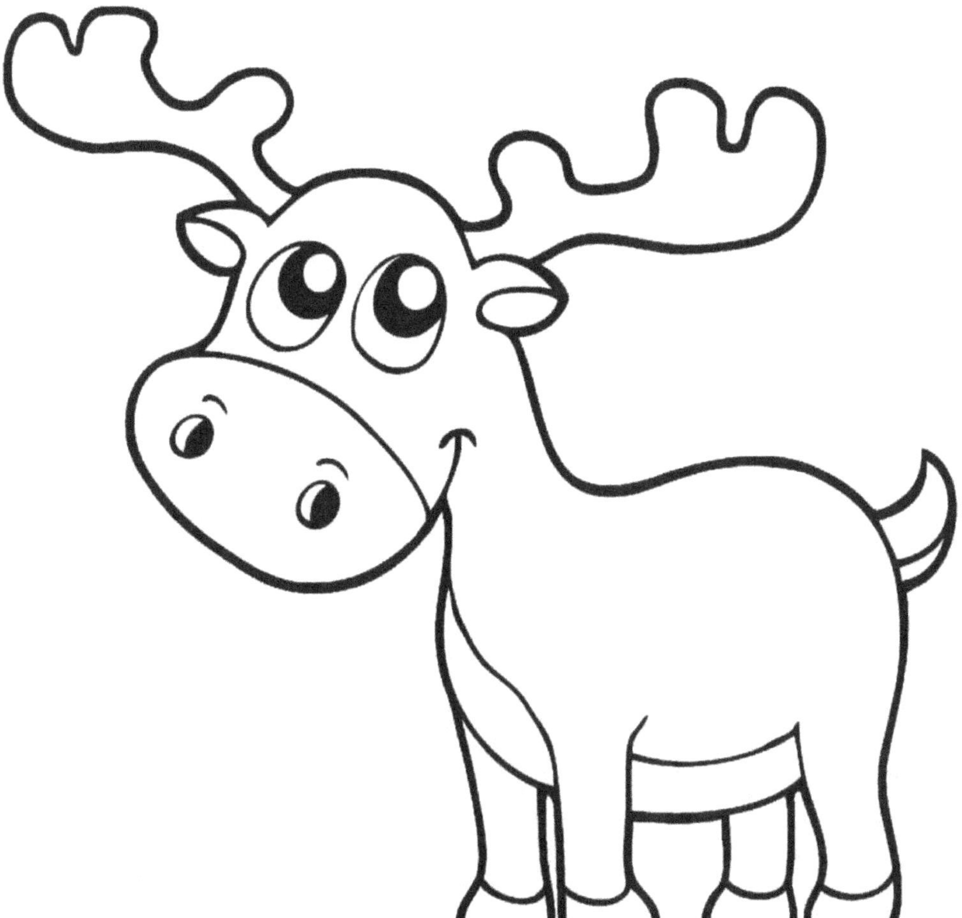

Reindeer

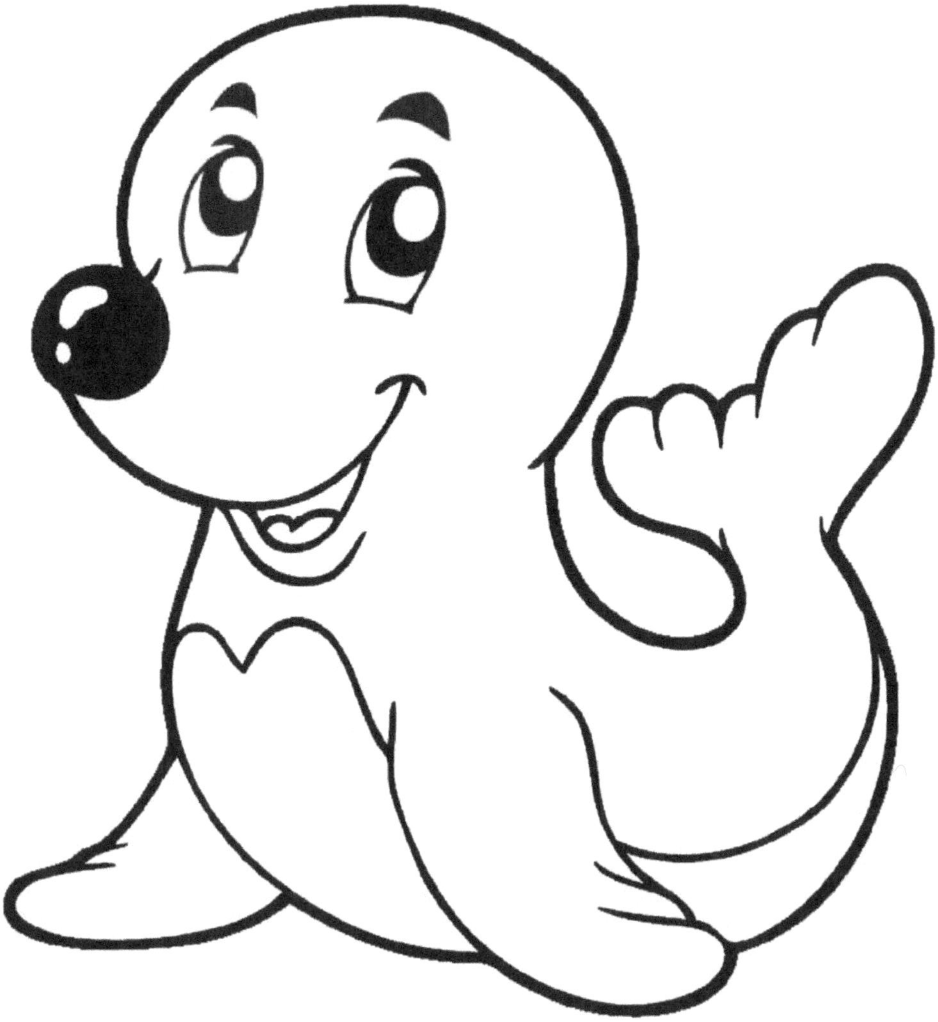

Seal

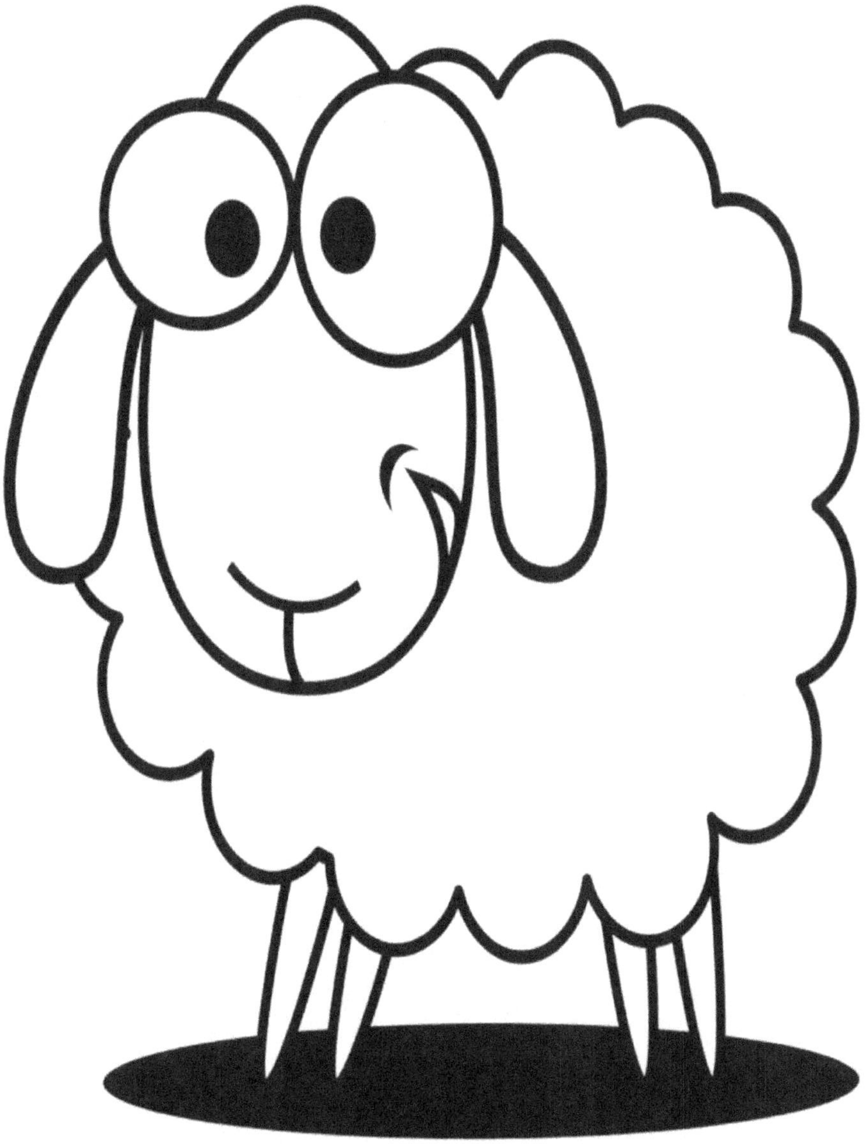

Sheep

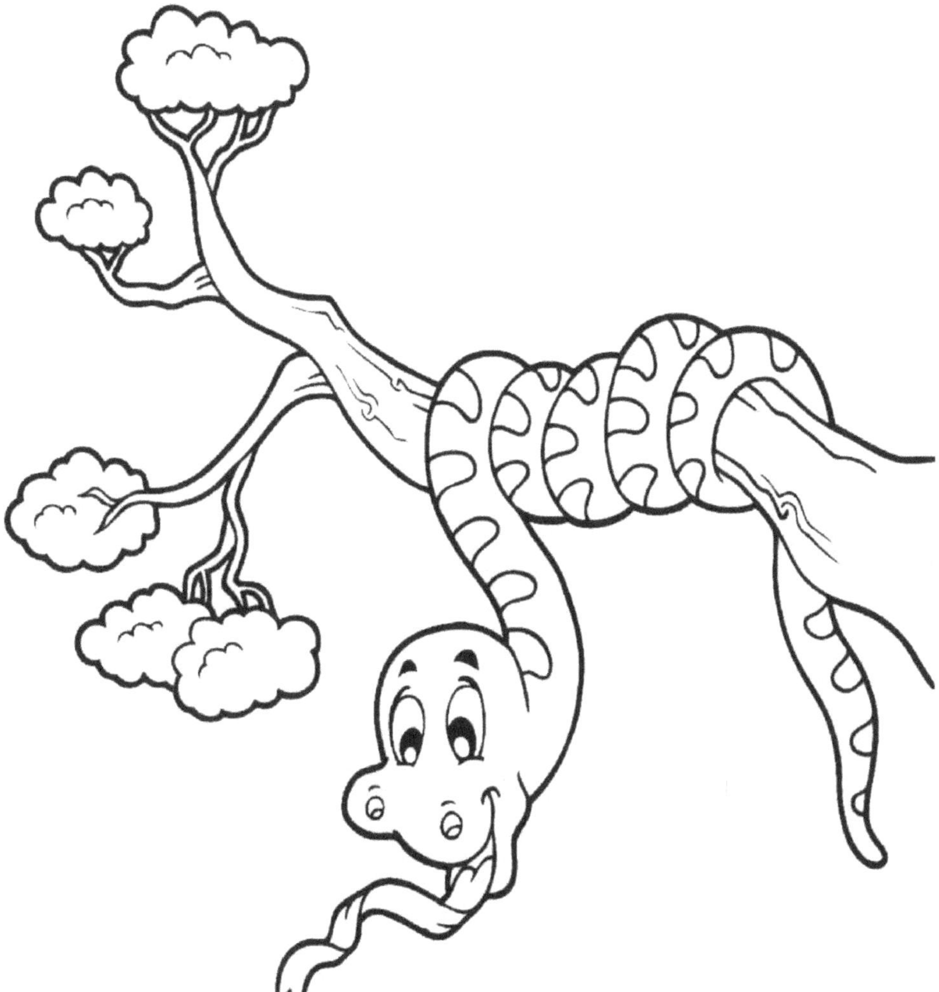

Snake

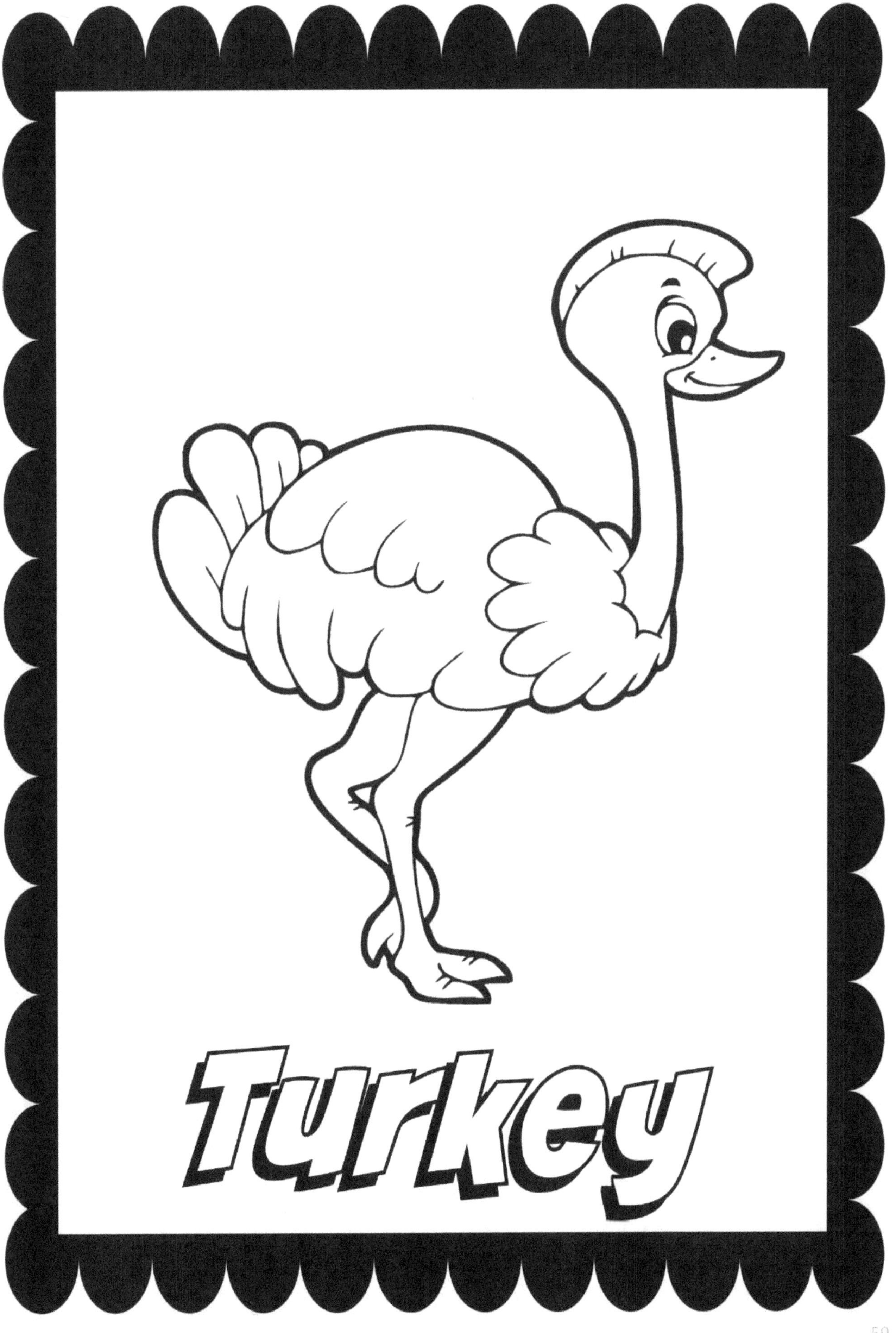
Turkey

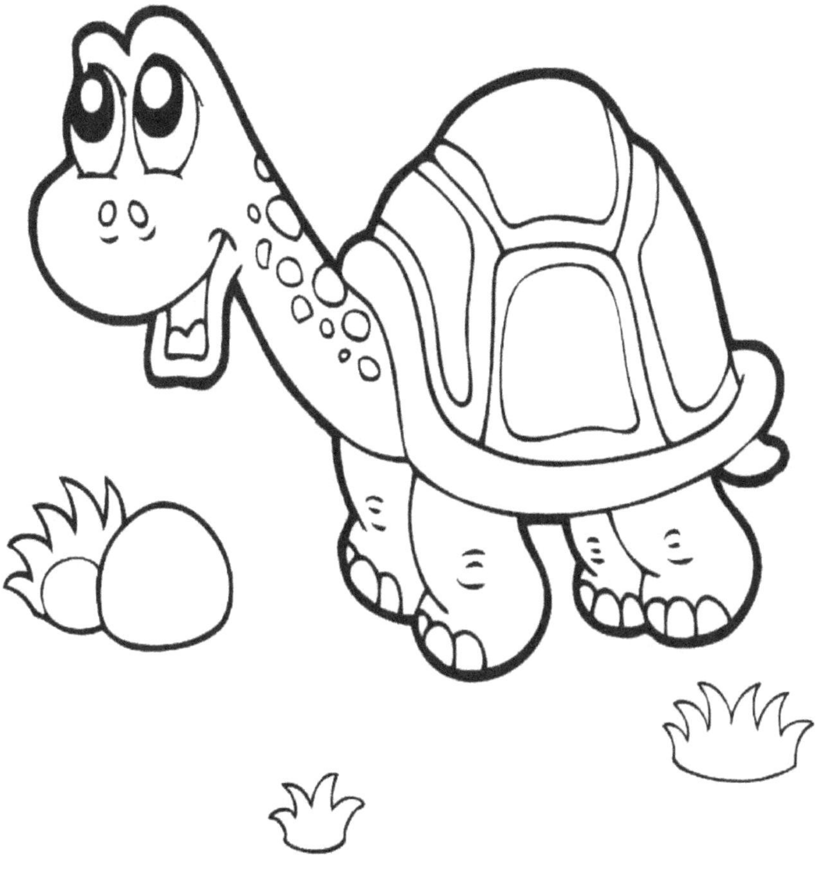

Turtle

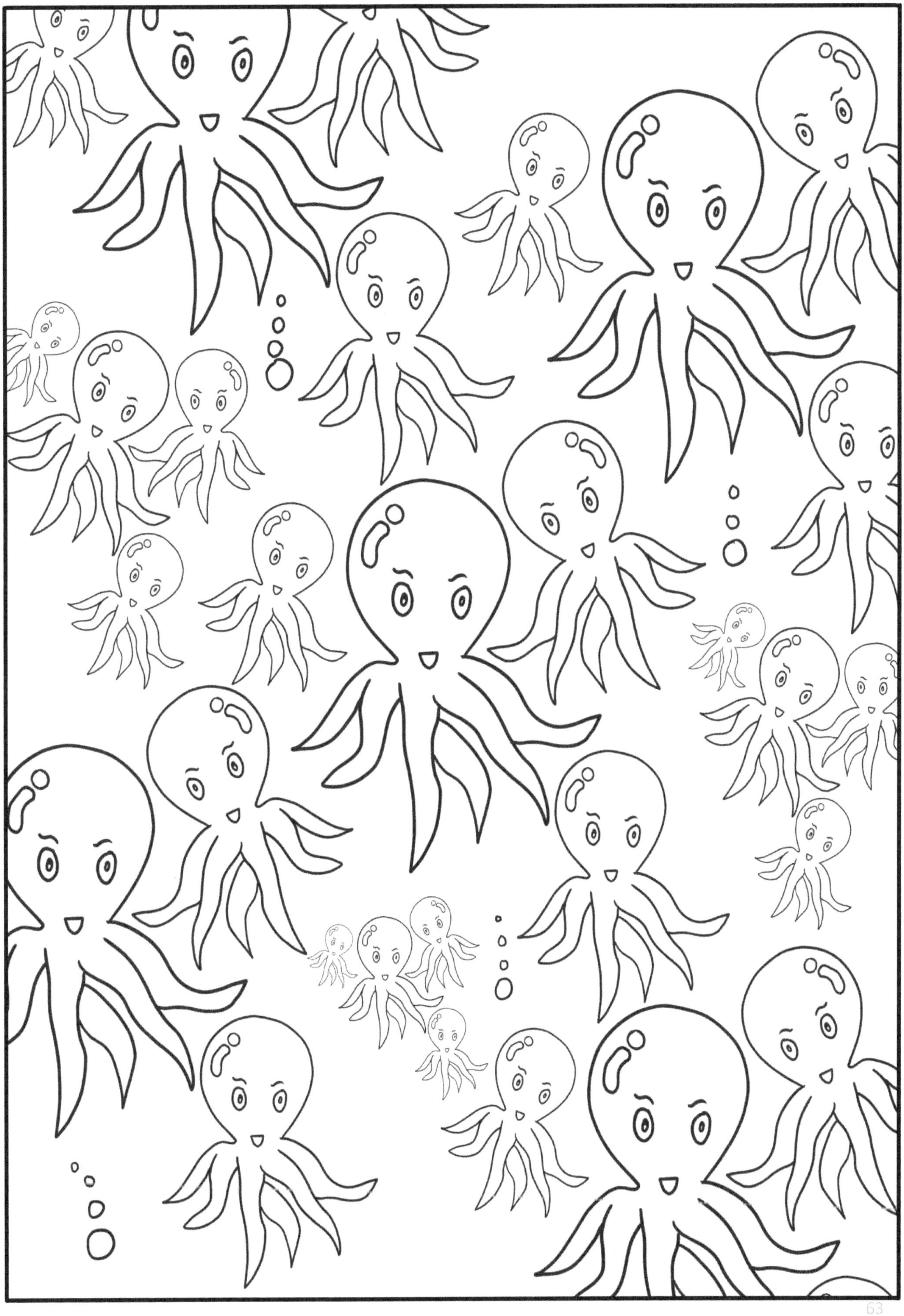

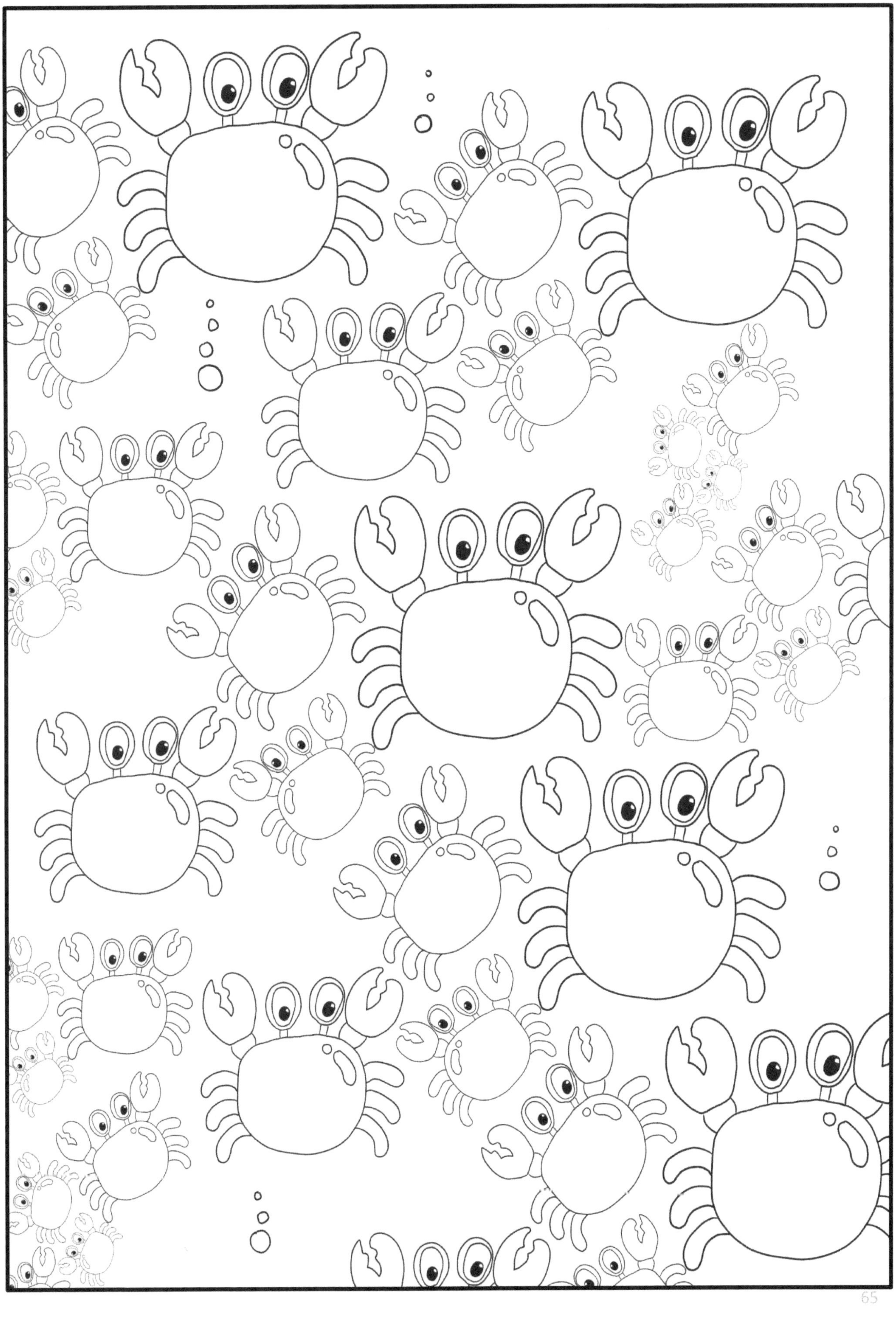

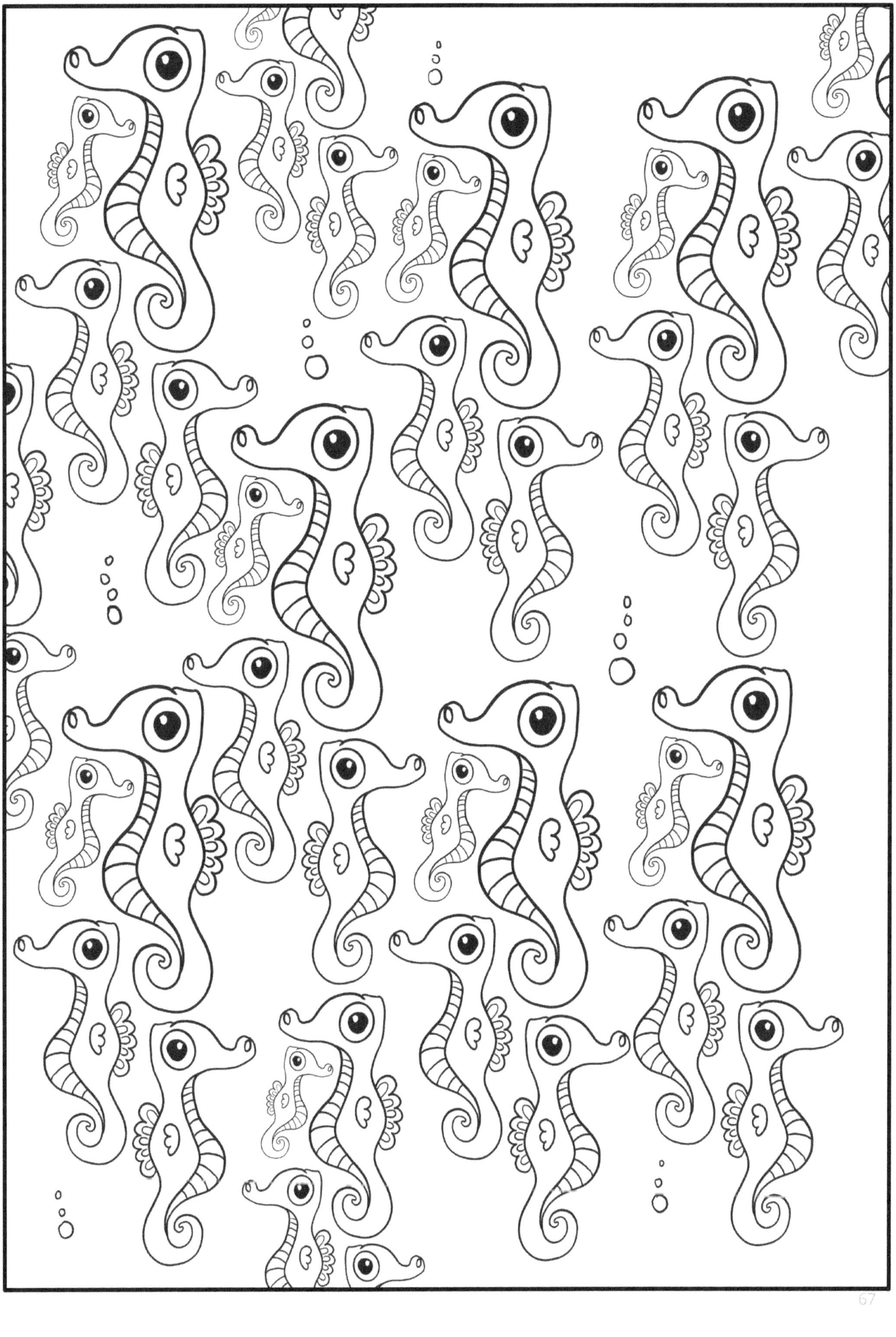

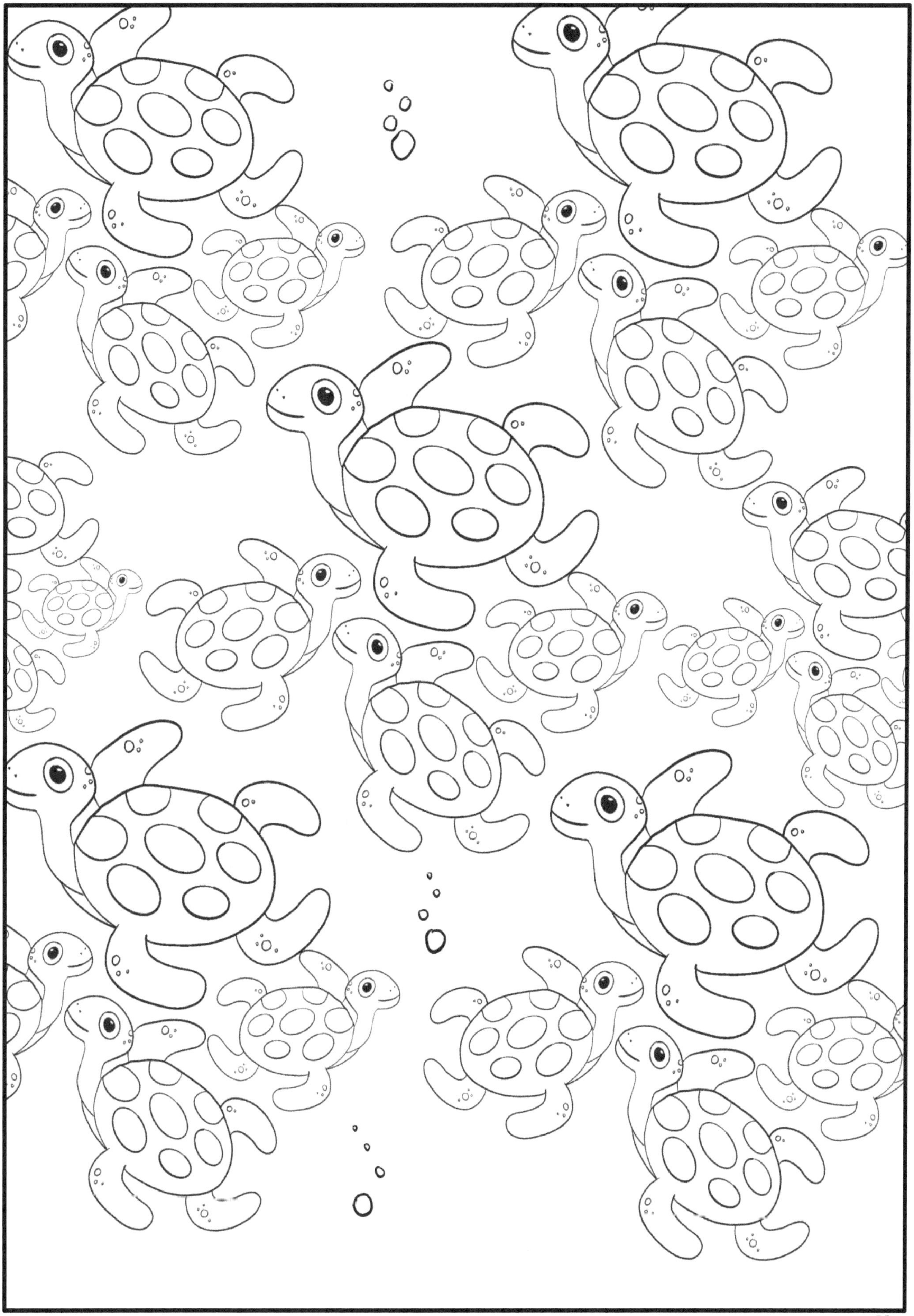

www.ingramcontent.com/pod-product-compliance
Lightning Source LLC
Chambersburg PA
CBHW082025230526
45466CB00023B/3383
* 9 7 9 8 5 8 7 7 6 3 5 0 0 *